"Poetry is a language that speaks to the heart, and Charles Ghigna uses that tender, heart-piercing language to bring us closer to his Southern soul. A collection as beautiful as it is heartfelt, *Southern Bred* transports and enchants."

— PATTI CALLAHAN HENRY

NYT Bestselling author of *The Secret Book of Flora Lea*

"You don't so much read these poems as fall into them. It's like plummeting into someone else's memories—a great rush of beauty and darkness, joy and weirdness. As soon as you finish one, you want to start over again from the beginning. This book is such a gift."

— GIN PHILLIPS

Author of *Fierce Kingdom* and *Family Law*

"With the gift of poetry, what he calls, "the field and stream of consciousness," Charles Ghigna has sketched a word portrait—indelible images both lovely and hard—of life in our rural, God-haunted South. In this memoir of verse, Ghigna makes clear, as he has before, that he is one of the finest poets of our time."

— FRYE GAILLARD

Author of *The Southernization of America*

"Ghigna's Southern voice comes through more palpably here than in anything I've read in a long while. I am already transported and in love with it. I keep waiting for sweet tea to just magically show up on my table."

— NIKKI GRIMES

Author of *Ordinary Hazards: A Memoir*

"I was utterly engrossed while reading *Southern Bred*, reliving every childhood memory, even though they weren't my own. I'll never understand how Charles Ghigna can evoke so much—a prick of tears, a knowing grin, memories of home, questions about life—with so few words. Yet he does it so beautifully."

— KELLY KAZEK

Author of *Southern Handbook*

"*Southern Bred* is a look back and a look forward, complete with honeysuckle and shadows, holy spaces and merciless stains. These poems alternately terrify and comfort, painting a captivating portrait of a boy, a poet, a man—and the indelible impact of the land and family to which one belongs. This collection is one of Charles Ghigna's best!"

— IRENE LATHAM

Author of *Leaving Gee's Bend*

"The poems in this collection move easily between dreams and waking life, situating themselves in that liminal space where insights arise, memories unfold, and time expands. In lucid language charged with meaning, Ghigna carries us along on ventures into the past that resist the sentimental and take us somewhere deeper: to the mysteries of fathers and sons, the suddenness of beauty, the surprise of death, and the holiness of life itself."

—JENNIFER HORNE

Former Alabama Poet Laureate and author of *Odyssey of a Wandering Mind*

SOUTHERN BRED

POEMS

CHARLES GHIGNA

central
avenue
2025

Copyright © 2025 Charles Ghigna
Cover and internal design © 2025 Central Avenue Marketing Ltd.

All rights reserved. No part of this book may be used or reproduced in any manner whatsoever without written permission from the author except in the case of brief quotations embodied in critical articles and reviews.

This is a work of fiction. Names, characters, places and incidents either are the product of the author's imagination or are used fictitiously and any resemblance to actual persons, living or dead, business establishments, events or locales is entirely coincidental.

Published by Central Avenue Poetry, an imprint of Central Avenue Marketing Ltd.
centralavenuepublishing.com

SOUTHERN BRED

Trade Paper: 978-1-77168-418-7
Ebook: 978-1-77168-419-4

Published in Canada
Printed in United States of America

1. Poetry / American

10 9 8 7 6 5 4 3 2 1

for Debra, always

Contents

I

Southern Bred	3
1952	4
Jimmy's Dad	5
Paper Planes	6
The Basement	7
Fish	8
Birthday Funeral	9
Riding to School	10
Southern Bin	11
In the Shadow of the Raven	12
Buck Dancing	13
Hunting Boys	14
Ever Green	15
Oak	16
Nature Trail	17

II

Signs	21
When Howard Became Jesus	22
Shop Class	24
Guilt Lifts Me Up	26
Nocturnal Roll Call	27
The House on the Cliff by the Sea	28
Spring Cleaning	29
Searching for the Field	30
Going All the Way	31
Day Dream	32
The Electrocution Complex	33
Falling Down Another Birthday Dream	34
Night Mare	36
Bull Rider	37
Over Herd	38

Brave New Whirl	39
Skydiving	40
Keeping Things Holy	42
Poem as Priest	44
Poem Hunter	45
The Balloon Poem	46
The Porcupine Poem	47

III

The Bass Fisherman	51
Pitching Horseshoes	52
Best Man	53
Riding Trains	54
The Bridge	55
Reunion	56
Speaking in Tongues	57
Samuel	58
Taking Turns	59
Cleaning Out the Closet	60
Dragon Death	62
Early Evening	65
Little Spaces	66

SOUTHERN BRED

I

SOUTHERN BRED

In the backyard
of my father's house
a hen's warm neck
once filled my pale fist.

Her place on the stump
still wears my shadow
like a stain.

1952

I was six
when they stuck me
inside the scrapbook
with a puppy in my lap.

Reopening it all now,
my hand touches
the truth of my father
who made me sit still
in that soft moment
when everything became
so neatly black and white.

JIMMY'S DAD

Jimmy's dad looked like an empty mailbox on a cloudy day.
He wore gray overalls and carried a red bandana
in his hip pocket that hung straight down like a windless flag.
He wore stiff black shoes and carried a metal lunch pail.
"James" sat over his shirt pocket announcing his name to the world.
Little strands of black thread unraveled from it like a spider.

On the way home from school we'd see him sitting
beside the pumps on an empty RC crate
cleaning his fingernails with a pocket knife
or over in the bay working under a car
with only his legs sticking out.

One day a Buick slipped off its jack and crushed him.
That's when Jimmy stopped coming to school.

PAPER PLANES

After his dad died
Jimmy invited me over
to spend the night
at his house.

On the wall
over his bed
hung a calendar
with a page for every day.

That night
we made paper planes
from the old day pages
of the calendar

just like Jimmy's dad
had taught him
before he went away
to live upon the dresser

in his little
silver frame house
whose shiny glass
window

became a target
for paper planes
that flew across the room
on folded yesterdays.

THE BASEMENT

Our basement smelled like damp ashes when it rained.
I played down there in the summer by myself.
I pretended I was a prisoner and the basement was my cell.
The furnace was a firing squad.
I wrapped the blindfold over my eyes, tied it tight, leaned back
against the concrete wall, and stretched out my arms in a cross.
I liked the way the wall felt cold and damp against my back.
I shut my eyes, whispered a prayer, and waited.
Sometimes I stayed quiet when Mom called.

FISH

August slipped in through the window
and slept heavy in my bed.
The sheets stuck to me like damp tape.
The old metal fan hummed a lullaby.
I turned my pillow over, propped it up,
and fell asleep reading Jack London.

Three children died beside the frozen lake today:
Charlie, Mick, and me.
It was after Charlie caught a fish through the hole in the ice.
By the time Mick arrived the fish had lost its flops and was frozen.
So was Charlie.

Mick put the fish in his pocket, pulled Charlie by the collar
across the lake like a sled, propped him up against a tree
and sat down beside him.
Little puffs of smoke like cartoon character balloons
floated out of Mick's mouth with each sigh.
Finally his eyes closed and the puffs stopped.
I walked over to the tree, put the fish in my pocket,
knelt in the snow and kissed them both on the cheek.
Then I sat down beside them and didn't get up.

BIRTHDAY FUNERAL

Two days before my birthday, my brother died.
They buried him in the Strayhorn Cemetery
under the oak that wore its Spanish moss like a tattered shawl.
It rained the night before and everything was sticky.

We all stood bent and wore gray clothes.
I stood behind Uncle Billy staring into the wool of his coat
thinking about how my brother was going to miss my birthday.
The coat moved and I heard someone crying.
Everyone's shoes were covered in mud.

When we got back home,
my cake was waiting in the middle of the kitchen table.
People kept coming in and leaving all day.
I sat in the kitchen staring at my cake,
thinking how it would taste even though I wasn't hungry.

RIDING TO SCHOOL

I sat in the car
watching the corn field
fan from my right eye.

With left eye shut,
I, the moving target,
took aim.

The giant fan spun
like a wheel whose center weight
was the field's unknown other side.

My father took me to school
because his father would not.
There was no way out.

Inside,
the trigger of a man
pulled tight.

SOUTHERN BIN

A mouse runs from under his board,
stops short, knows me.
The corn in his eyes turns gray.

IN THE SHADOW OF THE RAVEN

A breast of feathers,
purple black,
you swooped by
then circled back.

My shadow cast
upon the ground.
You landed there
without a sound

as if you knew
the morning sun
would show us how
we two are one.

BUCK DANCING

Two eight-point buck
lay beside the frozen lake,
their antlers locked
in a last dance.

It was their rite
to fight for dominance
in this, their final
rutting season,

to die for the doe
they would never know.
This was the hunting season
I searched through the cold

for the buck that would make me a man.
This was the season I found
by the lake my future frozen
for a moment in the snow.

HUNTING BOYS

It happens every year
from autumn to spring—
a dozen or so are lost,
good ole boys every one:
boys from Butler County,
Bibb, Clarke, and Cullman,
boys from Bullock and Clay,
boys who stay up late
every November evening
rubbing oil and dreams
into the steel of old guns,
boys who leave warm homes
to walk cold woods, forever.

EVER GREEN

Down, down, down again I go
into the hollows of the deep green forest,
into the untrodden damp green forest
where my soiled boot soles know

how cool green mornings can be,
how soily sweet the mud,
how slippery fresh each step,
step, step beneath the Ever Tree.

OAK

Like the steady face
of the flying squirrel,
I sail through the parting air

of falling leaves
and land at last
on the forest floor.

I scamper here and there
searching for the perfect acorn,
that little balm of time

that holds the tree of life
within its tiny seed,
that tempting core

I want so much to find,
that missing piece of me
I want so much to be.

NATURE TRAIL

These old steps
made from cut
railroad ties
lead me down
past the stump bench
to the stream
that flows
from the top
of the hill
and winds
past dogwood
poplar and pine
where I pause
to listen
to the wind
in the trees
to the babble
of the brook
to the owl
whose questions
go unanswered
to the hawk
who calls me out
to the dark
that calls me
home.

II

SIGNS

I am the back of the attic mirror.
From my side I see only out.
The change of seasons I once wore
leaves no reflection on me.

I wear my silver fleck in pieces
like the holey No Hunting sign
aired by the bully's bullets.
The wind whistles through, not at, me.

A parade of angry faces drives by
searching for the one with the reckless gun.
But they will not find me in this town
for I am attic bound.

My lead hides in the grass miles away.
My shell rusts in the weeds by the road.
I am attic faced in shadows.
I search through the dark for a sign.

WHEN HOWARD BECAME JESUS

No one in the huddle laughed
when Howard said he was Jesus,
that if we did not believe him
we were all sinners doomed to hell.
The next play was a hand-off to Howard.
Everyone, even our team, piled on,
grabbing for Howard, for the ball,
for the chance to cling to something solid.
When our boyhood heap had finally become still,
a pointed shadow drew our eyes way down the field
and there against the goal post leaned Howard,
the warm ball in his arms like a baby,
his eyes round and deep like the barrels of a gun.
Walking home, everyone was silent but Howard.
He said he had wanted to tell us about it before,
but was not sure we were ready to listen,
not sure we were ready to believe.
He said for the last year and a half
as he lay each night on his back,
his arms stretched out in a cross,
his feet so neatly together,
he was sure he had been chosen to lead us
in the path of righteousness for his namesake.
He said it was not luck that he had aced every test,
that the bookcase and birdhouse he built in shop class
won ribbons at the county fair.
He said that was just his way of being Jesus,
that we must learn to trust his perfect ways

and regard his saintly airs with adulation.
But we walked on in silence, each new step
so tight and full of fear we could not breathe,
could not break away and run on home alone.
At his house we stopped and watched him enter,
his eyes releasing us at last behind the door.
That night beside our beds we fell to prayer
and prayed that all that afternoon was just a dream,
that we would wake up in the morning and find Howard
in the huddle telling lies just like before.

SHOP CLASS

Like a row of little rubber ghosts,
the four pale Trojans stood stretched over
the bulbous wooden handles of the old lathe tools,
the wide shop class windows framing it all
in the warm glaze of the early autumn afternoon.
Howard held his breath beside me at the workbench,
his eyes nailing down the floor at our feet.
Most of us took shop for an easy grade.
With Howard it was different.
Howard liked the wood.
He liked the way the grain pulled his fingers
up and down each length of board.
He liked the fresh smell of the sawdust
as the whirling lathe breathed the wood
upon his hands, upon his handmade apron.
His lamps were the envy of us all,
standing straighter and brighter than the ones
made by the masterful hands of Mr. Tribble.
But today it was not the wood
that weighed upon our minds.
It was not the need to build an easy A.
Today it was the row of rubbers
that held us tight and stiff
in our dusty room of silence.
Howard, too, knew it was me who pulled the prank,
knew it was me who slipped into class before the bell
to do the dare, to decorate the sacred dais
of Mr. Tribble's trusty, ancient tools.

It was finally Howard's turn to talk,
to wear the stern shadow that came to stand
one by one over our bowed heads,
the Inquisition of one who came to each of us
to ask if we had committed the cardinal sin.
Howard, my best friend, raised his eyes, looked at me, lied,
and whispered, "*Yes.*"

GUILT LIFTS ME UP

Guilt tiptoes
down the hall,
turns right
into the bedroom
of my dreams.

I pull the blanket
over my head,
but Guilt finds me,
lifts me up
to the ceiling,

through the ceiling
to the night sky
past the treetops
into the canopy of stars
that shine their way

to the other side
of my nightmare
that begs the morning light
to come break through
this gray curtain of Guilt.

NOCTURNAL ROLL CALL

In the evening
when the shadows have all crawled
so far across my room they become my room,

something calls names in the night.
It comes from the garden,
from inside the roses,

from out of the earth
through its cool roots,
from out of that place

where the cicada sings.
The sound shakes the house,
my room, this bed,

the red in my shut eyes.
But it is not the locust
or his cry that frightens me.

It is not the rose
that grips the ground with every tick.
It is the sound I do not hear

that haunts my nights.
It calls all names in this dark room,
but never mine.

THE HOUSE ON THE CLIFF BY THE SEA

I come Ishmael to you from the midnight sea.
The gray fog clings, a pasted beard, to my cheeks.
It grows wild from my chin around the world.

You raise the lantern
higher to your face
and stare into the dark at a dream.

The window holds you
like a portrait hung against the sky.
I come bringing morning in my beard.

SPRING CLEANING

First signs of life
and we stand in a bed of weeds
pulling up wild vines in the sun.

The honeysuckle holds
tight to the house,
bracing itself against the red brick,

but we have come for it all,
we have come to clear the way,
marching side by side into spring,

into this season that pulls us out
of ourselves and lets us hold life
in our hands by the roots.

SEARCHING FOR THE FIELD

Sunday, and we drive past the last building
to where its shadow no longer touches the car.
We stare at the broken line until it becomes earth

and listen to the crickets when we stop.
We join them in their singing, filling
our lungs with pine and magnolia.

We lie down in a bed of clover
and watch the moon on its way to morning.
We sleep until the sun warms our dreams,

until the firm hand of a kindhearted farmer
helps us back to our feet, until the trust
of his grip sends us on our way back home

to the buildings, to the shadows,
to the broken yellow line
that sent us searching for this field.

GOING ALL THE WAY

It is an afternoon in mid July
when we finally do the dare,
run full-tilt across the field,

close our eyes, leap into the sky—
and we are up and over the shadows,
above the weight of summer's heat,

flying like we've always dreamed of doing,
arms stretched out into wings,
hair blown back in waves of silk,

rising and falling and rising again,
freer than we have ever been,
wishing we could bring back to earth

what we have known in dreams,
in all those times like this
before we learned to trust our eyes.

DAY DREAM

Childhood,
and again
I am outside

on a hilltop
staring up
at the clouds

searching past the cumulus
to the long-tail dragons
and silver sailing ships

that have come to take me away
to this rare dream
of dreaming.

THE ELECTROCUTION COMPLEX

I dream I am sitting in a white room
staring at a two-way mirror
wondering who is

watching on the other side
of the silvered glass.
I see my face floating up

like a farewell balloon,
like a Munch portrait
with no hands.

Steel bandana in place,
copper bracelets at my wrists,
I lock my final stare upon the wall

until the wall becomes a window,
until the window becomes a room,
until the room becomes a room without walls.

FALLING DOWN ANOTHER BIRTHDAY DREAM

Inside this old wooden house of me
someone falls backwards down my stairs,
not as in an August nightmare

or a drive-in movie,
but backwards
down the steps I've yet to take.

Sometimes the faller is a friend
whose face is broad and smiling,
a fishing rod in one hand, waving with the other;

sometimes the faller is a woman in shorts,
her hands full of lipsticks and mirrors;
sometimes the faller is my father,

his strong hand reaching for the banister,
his sharp voice calling for help
with the wake-up shout

that sent me to school on time;
sometimes the faller is a priest
whose fall is muted and slow-motioned

as though under water behind a wall of glass;
and sometimes the faller is me,
older, younger, innocent and brave,

falling backwards
on purpose,
with purpose.

NIGHT MARE

Inside this horse I ride
there is no horse.
She saddles me to her

because she thinks she is.
Silent, softer than cream,
we canter on midnight.

Doorway shadows of locked shops
lure us, become each
new night's mare.

Dark windows mark our way
with windy strips of velour
as we press on and on

through the city,
chasing our dreams
into morning.

BULL RIDER

I grip the leather
with my left hand
and hammer my fist
with my fist.

The sweat of my palm
soaks through the leather glove
into the patient,
waiting rein.

The beast below
bucks in his stall,
reminds me
he is not as tame

as his brothers and sisters
who stand in line
waiting to become
the glove, hat, wallet,

dinner, belt, boots
of this stranger
who holds in his hand
a piece of the final meld.

OVER HERD

This time it will be different.
This time I will not follow
my bovine brothers

one by one down the ramp,
head first through the chute
into the slaughterhouse,

into the waiting slug of night.
This time I will rouse the herd,
I will rise from my dung

drenched funeral boards,
I will sway from side to side
in my heavy wave of defiance,

I will dance my rite to life,
I will rock and roll this cattle car
right off its clacking tracks.

BRAVE NEW WHIRL

I drift in a nether world
between now and then
where time is a river

that drowns the night,
where memory purls easy over ice
and rocks my lies to sleep,

where slices of truth, ripe as morning,
sit on the salty edge
of this brave new whirl.

SKYDIVING

First step
and I swallow
the dry, delicious fear
of walking on air.

Body bent back
into a bow,
I fall into the arms
of the screaming wind,
my heart beating taps
in my ears.

Pop,
and an angel wing
pulls me from the thunder
of a hundred-
mile-an-hour dream.

I sit perched,
a runaway cloud
of contentment,
a fearless eagle feather
lost in the drift
of an early afternoon.
Knees bent, I pull
the taut reins of reality,
ready-set myself
for one final little lift,

one last tiptoe of air
before my flying feet
must run their
earthbound way
back home.

KEEPING THINGS HOLY

for Mark Strand

In a church
I am the absence
of church.

This is
always
the case.

Wherever I am
I am
what is missing.

When I walk
I part
the sacred air

and always
the blessed air
moves in

to fill
the spaces
where my body's been.

We all
have reasons
for moving.

I move
to keep things
holy.

POEM AS PRIEST

Like the good Catholic boy
who tells his all
to the patient priest,

I pour my soul
into my poem,
confess my passions,

my private fears
that flow like lamb's blood
upon this pure white page

that passes sentence
after sentence
upon my sins

and turns my
penance
into prayer.

POEM HUNTER

With pen for gun
I enter the field
and stream
of consciousness.

THE BALLOON POEM

I search
for another
balloon to fill,

one puff
after another
after another

until all
my hot air
is out,

until my tongue
tastes of talc
and rubber,

until another idea
comes red and swollen
and ready to burst.

THE PORCUPINE POEM

A porcupine can raise its quills, turn around,
and run backwards into its prey.

Just when I think
I am done with it,
my poem turns on me,

charges back for more,
pricks me with its
finer points,

reminds me
things are not
what they seem,

that the past is not past
until it turns and shows
its sharp, uncompromising side.

III

THE BASS FISHERMAN

in memory of my father

He was the silent type, the mute scholar
reading the sky instead of his books,
wasting no words above the still waters,
searching instead for shades of detail,
for the sharp, deep shadows of silver,
for the subtle moves that only seers see.

He was the careful type, the peaceful brave
wrapping his weapon with string, down
and prayer, warming his sight with colors
of sunset, waiting for sunrise to show him
the way, watching the depth of each cloud
that floated on the lake of his eyes.

He was the simple type, the timeless boy
flipping and testing his first flying rod,
urging it on past limits of hand and arm
to the other side of vision and dreams,
using all of that first moment to cast
the perfect balance of boy and boat.

He was the cautious type, the prize bass
with the broken hook still in his mouth,
staring up at the lake's final surface of man,
following the drag of the feather's taunt,
waiting, waiting, learning at last
the only reward of patience, is patience.

PITCHING HORSESHOES

in memory of my father

They came from their homes,
Black Labels sweating in their palms,
to test their skill, their luck,

their moment in the sun
against the one
who made the horseshoes ring;

men whose only play was here
in this side yard Sunday ritual
where summer flew on the weight

and promise of each pitch,
where winter seemed a stranger
in the eyes of the smiling young fathers

who came to stake their claim
against the one they called The Ringer,
the one who tosses still within my dreams.

BEST MAN

in memory of my father

Flown in round and grinning, holding out
the stronger hand in every stranger's shake,
kissing all the women on the hand.
To me he was more than just a father.
Perhaps it was the way he wore his tuxedo
or the way it turned his temples silverfox.
His cheeks were full and glowing,
smiling for me and my bride through it all,
through the starchy reminder of last year's
two attacks on his heart, going home to one more,
to the dreaded grip of an early retirement,
breathing Catholic hard beside me
in that Southern Baptist church,
wading through the thick smiles to the car,
to the small airport at the end of the dream.

Home, remembering it all before dawn,
enjoying in sleep the proud son image again,
almost touching my shoulder for luck.
Rising, staring past the shouting clock
set the night before by some brutal hand of habit.

RIDING TRAINS

A boy is trapped inside
my skin holds its color
like the face of the watch
Father kept in his pocket
played the same tune
no matter the place
the time we rode
the train without speaking
all the way to Washington
and back we talked
about the knot
in my Cub Scout
handkerchief
and what I would
think about riding trains
when I grew up.

THE BRIDGE

There is no water,
no deep ravine,
but there are footsteps
on my bridge.

I hear them at night
crossing slowly
like weary soldiers
home from a final battle,

like the footsteps
of my father
who came each night
to see I was asleep,

like the footsteps of my son
who stands in the dark
calling for water
in my dreams.

REUNION

It happens in airports.
Glancing up from your phone,
you see them embrace,
see them hold on to each other
as though their lives
depended upon it,
as though the whisper
of each other's name
could keep them alive.

But this time it is you
who flew north
to the snowy funeral
of your namesake,
you who hugs this
stranger of ten years,
you who calls her *sister*
in a voice that sounds
foreign to you, to her,
to the people
looking up
from their phones.

SPEAKING IN TONGUES

for Andrew Hudgins

Like their fathers before them,
our fathers said nothing of love;
yours with the kicking bull

whose tail got out of hand,
mine with the pet pullet
whose proud neck stained my fist.

That was the way of our fathers.
No one told them of such things.
No one gave them the trinity of words.

We hold the tongues
of our fathers, still; a silence
we will not hold against our sons.

SAMUEL

I place old boards, a used tire
and a broken umbrella beside the road
for Samuel who comes in his pickup
before the county cleanup truck arrives.

But it is the mother, sister
beast, bird who feeds us,
rarely the father, brother.

Samuel waves at the house, smiles
into the early sun,
his gold tooth gleaming.

On the porch a tired Katy
licks the last of her litter,
leans back on her side,
waits to be suckled.

Across the road in a quiet pasture
Possum nurses her calf
while here in the kitchen
I break tradition again
and shovel a spoonful of grits
into my stubborn son.

TAKING TURNS

Father died.
Mother died.
Their ashes in me
burn.

The wind blew.
I spread a few
from the golden
urn.

I stood and sighed.
A crow cried
its echo
in return.

The sky turned blue
then I knew
the earth would take
its turn.

CLEANING OUT THE CLOSET

Sometimes I wish my past
were the corner of my closet,
a soft, familiar place
where I could stretch out
and lie down on all my worn-out shoes,
a place where I could step back in
and tell all my baseball buddies
I'm sorry for lying and nodding *yes*
when we told stories
about going all the way,
a place where I could retake
all my college tests,
a place where I could recapture
my promise of pitching for the Pirates,
a place where I could rewrite
all my published poems,
a place where I could keep my parents
as young as their wedding pictures,
a place where I could tell them
I love them, tell my sisters I love them,
tell them I wish they had a place
in the corner of their closets like mine
where we could go together
to say and do all the things
our distance never let us do,
a private place where all our regrets
hang like old suits in the dark,
a place where we could put them on again,

one by one, and never wear them out,
and never wear them out.

DRAGON DEATH

Old Dragon Death,
Old Dragon Death,
I beseech you
to take me on,
to raise your wicked head
once more and blow
your fiery breath
into my hearth,
into the heart that you have
already slain in the name
of my beloved family.

How dare you rage against
all I love and leave me alone.
How dare you carry my father
into the fire of World War II,
return him home a hollow shell
of the young hero he once was,
burning his dreams to ashes,
gnawing away his leg
forty years later,
leaving him a sad invalid
to sit in a stuffed chair and stare
out the window in fear
wondering where on earth
you are hiding,
where you will be rising next,
watching the evening news

for signs of your daily scourge.
How dare you rumble
into his living room
three years later
and take the rest of him away,
his ashes spilling
from the corners of your mouth
onto the mountain he loved.

How dare you drag your monster tail
across my mother's eyes,
leaving her alone
in the house to stare at the walls
of medals and memories,
returning nine years later
before the dawn of Mother's Day
to suck the sweet life
from the woman who taught me
to love, to dream, to see through
the shadows to the light
that shines from within,
to smile in the face of the deadly dragon,
to slay him with my sword of life,
to chop him into pieces
with the passion
of all I have known,
of all I have cherished and lost
to the deadly dragon
who always returns.

I am finished with this warning.

I am finished with these words
I waste on you.
I am ready.
Now come for me,
you son of a bitch,
come for me.

EARLY EVENING

inspired by the painting "Boys in a Dory, 1873" by Winslow Homer

We are rowing our way
across this small, stretched
canvas of time

into the shadows
of a watercolored world
where we float as in a dream,

soft and serene,
beyond the touch of our master's hand
into the final stroke of everlasting light.

LITTLE SPACES

Little spaces.
Tiny traces.
That's what
I look for.

Shady spots.
Small clay pots.
Garden walls
without a door.

Hiding places
with no faces
where the world
cannot find me.

In my tree house
like a free mouse—
that's where I most
want to be.

Charles Ghigna is a poet, and children's author, and nationally syndicated feature writer. He is the author of more than 5,000 poems and one hundred books for children and adults ranging from the 1990 Pulitzer Prize nominee *Returning to Earth* to the popular children's book *The Father Goose Treasury of Poetry for Children*. His books have been published by Disney, Random House, Scholastic, Simon & Schuster and others. His poems for adults have been published in *Harper's, The New Yorker, Rolling Stone, The Saturday Evening Post* and *The Wall Street Journal*. His poems for children appear in *Highlights for Children, Cricket, Ranger Rick, Humpty Dumpty, Jack and Jill, Spider, Ladybug, Babybug, Caterpillar, Children's Digest* and *The School Magazine*.

Ghigna served as poet-in-residence at the Alabama School of Fine Arts, instructor of creative writing at Samford University, and has received fellowship grants and various awards and recognitions from the John F. Kennedy Center for the Performing Arts, the Mary Roberts Rinehart Foundation, the Rockefeller Brothers Fund, the National Endowment for the Arts, and the Library of Congress. A popular speaker at schools, colleges, conferences, and libraries, Ghigna has spoken at the American Library in Paris, the American International Schools in the Americas in South America and Alaska, and at other events throughout the U.S. and overseas. For more information please visit CharlesGhigna.com